THE HISTORY OF
ELECTRICITY

ROBERT SNEDDEN

Thomson Learning
New York

CONTENTS

First published in the United States in 1995 by Thomson Learning, 115 Fifth Avenue, New York, NY 10003

First published in 1994 by Wayland (Publishers) Limited

Library of Congress Cataloging-in-Publication
Snedden, Robert.
    The history of electricity / Robert Snedden.
        p.   cm.—(Science discovery)
    Includes bibliographical references and index.
    ISBN 1-56847-250-1
        1. Electricity–History—Juvenile literature. [1. Electricity–History.]
    I. Title. II. Series. III. Series: Science discovery (New York, N.Y.)
    QC527.S69   1994
    537—dc20   94-34452

Printed in Italy

Acknowledgments
Concept David Jefferis
Text editor and picture research Michael Brown
Illustrations Robert Burns and James Robins
Cover design Norman Berger, U.S.A.

Picture credits
Bruce Coleman Ltd. 15 (B)
Delta Archive 6, 8, 9(TL), 12, 15(TL), 16(TL), 20, 23, 24, 25(TR), 26, 30, 31, 32, 35, 36(B), 37, 47
Mary Evans Picture Library 16 (BL)
Science Photo Library 4, 9(TR), 11, 13, 14, 19, 25, 27, 28, 29, 39, 40, 41, 45
The Science Museum 36(TR)
Cover: Van de Graaff generator; courtesy of the *New York Power Authority*.

☀ INTRODUCTION

Electricity is often taken for granted. We press a button or a switch and the television set comes on, a light shines, or the oven heats up. Most of us flick that switch without stopping to think about what happens when we do so, but how does electricity work? How is it made? What exactly is it?

Some of the effects of the linked forces of electricity and magnetism have been known for thousands of years. However, it was a long time before people began to examine these forces in a truly scientific manner. In this book we follow the steps of the scientists who have pieced together the puzzle of electricity. We will also see how the practical benefits that electricity gives us came about and look at some of the inventions that made electricity useful.

Even today there are new developments, and we finish off the book with a look at some possibilities for the future.

▶ The power of electricity allows colorful neon lighting in cities worldwide.

WHAT IS ELECTRICITY?

Learning about electricity requires knowing a little about the structure of matter itself. Everything in the universe – the stars, the planets, this book, your body – is made up of invisibly small atoms.

Each atom has a central nucleus that is surrounded by even smaller particles, called electrons, orbiting the nucleus. A material that passes electricity easily, such as a metal, is called a conductor. Conductors have "free" electrons moving outside the others. When a metal wire is connected to a battery, the free electrons drift along the wire, moving from atom to atom. This movement of electrons is called an electric current.

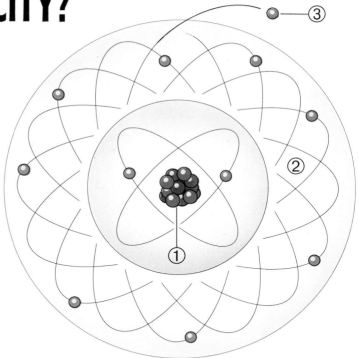

▲ **An atom. Its central nucleus (1), is surrounded by electrons (2), and a free electron (3).**

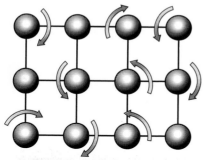

◀ **Atoms form a strong, regular pattern in metals. Normally, free electrons move from atom to atom at random.**

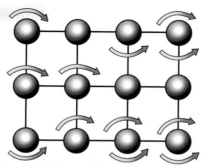

▶ **When a metal wire is joined to a power source such as a battery, free electrons drift in one direction as a current. There has to be a complete path to and from the battery. This is called a circuit. If the circuit is broken, the current stops immediately.**

The study of current electricity and magnetic fields is called electrodynamics. There is another type of electricity in which there is no regular flow as such. Instead, electrons build up in one place; hence the name static electricity. Examples of static electricity include thunderstorms and other natural phenomena where friction transfers electrons from one object to another. The study of this is called electrostatics.

It is impossible to imagine how tiny atoms and electrons are. To take an example, the current flowing through the glowing filament of an ordinary lightbulb consists of about a septillion (10^{24}) electrons a second!

This knowledge, simple as it seems, has taken a long time to piece together. The story begins back in the days of ancient Greece.

ELEKTRON AND LODESTONE

The people of ancient Greece knew of a yellow resin produced by some types of trees. They called this resin *elektron*, a substance we know today as amber. When amber sets hard it can be used for jewelry and ornaments. The Greeks, among them the great scientist Thales of Miletus (625?-547 B.C.), found that when amber was rubbed by fur or a piece of cloth it acquired a strange ability. Hair, feathers, and other small pieces of material were attracted to the amber and stuck to it by a force that we know today as static electricity. Thales is often considered to be the founder of science. He was the first recorded person to try to make sense of the world without employing myth and legend for explanations. He was a great astronomer and could calculate when a solar eclipse would take place.

▶ **You can create static electricity by rubbing a balloon with a dry cloth. The balloon will then attract small pieces of paper.**

Thales was also aware of the properties of the lodestone, a mineral containing iron, which is a strong natural magnet. Thales was the first person who was known to have studied magnetism, but as far as we know he didn't make a connection between the attractive properties of amber and lodestone. Other early thinkers on electricity and magnetism include the Roman philosopher Lucretius (100?-55? B.C.), who realized that iron filings gathered in a regular pattern near a magnet. But it was not until the sixteenth century that serious studies began.

▲ **Iron filings gather around the two ends, or poles, of a bar magnet. In doing so, they reveal the shape of the bar's magnetic field.**

▶ **William Gilbert**

Even if it was not understood how lodestone worked, there was a good use for it. If a lodestone shaped like a thin bar or a needle was allowed to move freely, either floating in water on a piece of wood or suspended from a cord, it always pointed in a roughly north-south direction. It could be used to find which way a traveler was going, and this was the discovery that led to the invention of the compass. Vikings used lodestones on their raiding and exploring voyages, and by A.D. 1200 the compass was a regular navigation tool for sailors.

William Gilbert (1544-1603), English court physician to Queen Elizabeth I, wrote a book called *De Magnete*, or *About Magnets*. Published in 1600, it put forward the theory that Earth was a giant lodestone, with north and south magnetic poles. This book was a compilation of everything that was known at that time about electricity and magnetism. Gilbert, in fact, was the first person to use the word *electricity*, from the Greek *elektron*. He suggested that electricity and magnetism were actually aspects of the same force. He also pointed out the difference between amber and lodestone: amber could attract any light material, but lodestone could only attract iron. Although Gilbert couldn't explain the things he described, his work provided a real starting point for the study of electricity.

 ## MAGNETIC POLES

Gilbert's work continued that of Peter Peregrinus, who wrote about magnets in 1269. Peregrinus noticed that magnetic needles pointed toward Earth's poles, so the ends of a magnet were named north and south poles. He also saw that unlike poles attracted and like poles repelled, and that if a magnet were cut in half, there would be two magnets instead of one.

ELECTRIC MACHINES

Otto von Guericke (1602-86) was a teacher who lived in the town of Magdeburg, Germany. He knew William Gilbert's work and tried to test Gilbert's idea that magnetism might be the force of attraction between stars and planets. In 1665 he made a sphere to represent Earth. At that time people thought Earth was made largely of sulfur (since this was a material found in volcanoes) so this was the material from which von Guericke made his sphere. The ball was attached to an axle so that it could be rotated using a hand crank. Von Guericke found that if he let his hand brush the ball lightly as it spun around it produced fairly sizable sparks. Soon others were finding ways to produce this new phenomenon, which was called "statical electricity," a term since shortened to static.

In the 1730s, Charles du Fay (1698-1739), superintendent of gardens for the king of France and a keen chemist, experimented with transferring electric charges to different objects by touching them with a static-charged glass rod. He discovered that sometimes charged objects were attracted to each other and sometimes they were repelled. Du Fay thought that there must be two different electrical "fluids" – he called them vitreous and resinous electricity – each type attracting the other but repelling itself. He also showed that the human body could be electrified as long as it was insulated from the ground.

▼ In 1729 British physicist Stephen Gray discovered that electricity could travel through certain materials. He is shown here sending an electric charge along a line of rope.

▲ Pieter van Musschenbroek with a Leyden jar apparatus. He rubbed the sphere to build up a static charge. The jar was charged at the end of the bar.

▶ A more up-to-date way of storing static charges was developed by American scientist Robert Van de Graaff in the 1930s. Vast charges of electricity can be built up in the metal sphere of the Van de Graaff generator.

 INSULATORS AND CONDUCTORS

Conductors are materials that pass electricity easily. Examples include metals such as copper and iron. Insulators are materials that do not pass electricity easily. Examples include glass, wax, and rubber.

In 1745 Ewald von Kleist, a priest from Pomerania (now part of Germany), experimented with a device for storing electricity. It was a glass jar partly filled with water and sealed with a cork that had a nail running through the middle and into the water. By touching the nail to a static electricity generator, von Kleist found that he could store the charge in the jar. Touching the charged nail to another object produced a strong spark as the jar discharged the electricity it had stored. Pieter van Musschenbroek of Leyden University, Holland, followed up von Kleist's experiments with great success. Soon many scientists were experimenting with the jars, which were called Leyden jars after the university. Before long, no self-respecting laboratory was without one.

American statesman Benjamin Franklin (1706-90) was one of these investigators. He realized that the spark from a Leyden jar might be connected with some much larger sparks.

☀ DOWN TO EARTH

When Benjamin Franklin looked at a discharging Leyden jar, he was reminded of a miniature lightning flash. Could the two actually be the same thing, but on vastly different scales? He set down his reasons for thinking that lightning was a form of electricity: it gave out light, it moved swiftly, and it was conducted by metals. He concluded, "They agree in all the particulars in which we can compare them. Let the experiment begin."

In June 1752, Franklin went out with his son into a field near Philadelphia to fly a kite in a thunderstorm. The kite had a pointed wire attached to it, to which Franklin tied a silk thread that would be charged by any electricity that was overhead. On the end of the silk thread was a key. As the lightning flashed above him Franklin put his hand near the key, drawing sparks from it. He also found that he could charge up a Leyden jar with the key, proving that lightning was a form of electricity. However, Franklin was a very lucky man. When a man named Professor Richmann of St. Petersburg, Russia, tried the same experiment, his assistant saw "a glow of blue fire as large as his fist" flash to the professor's head from his kite, killing him instantly.

① ② ③

◀▶ The lightning bolt is one of nature's most dramatic spectacles. It occurs when storm clouds gather and the water and ice particles inside them bump together. The bumping causes static electricity to build up. Positive charges collect in the highest clouds, and negative charges in the lower (1), with a small positive charge in the lowest clouds. When the buildup of charges is too great, a flash of lightning is released (2) – either from the bottom to the top of the cloud or from the bottom to the ground. When the negatively charged stroke nears the ground, it attracts a positive stroke from the point it will strike. When the strokes meet, they form a very bright return stroke which passes to the cloud. Here the church's lightning rod is struck (3), saving the building from damage.

Franklin thought of a practical benefit from his experiments, suggesting that metal rods be attached to the sides of tall buildings with wires leading into the ground. Such a conductor would carry an electrical discharge safely to earth, protecting the building from damage.

Franklin proposed that rather than there being two kinds of electricity, as du Fay had suggested, there was just one. An object with excess electric fluid was "positive" and attracted objects with little electric fluid, which were "negative." Electricity would move from the positive to the negative. Later research showed that Franklin, although wrong in thinking that electricity was a fluid, was right in principle.

In 1785 Charles Coulomb (1736-1806), a French physicist, showed that the force of attraction between electrically charged objects changed according to distance, reducing as the objects were moved apart.

CONDUCTING LIGHTNING

Franklin's experiments, dangerous as they were, provided much useful information as to the nature of lightning and natural electricity. Franklin's lightning conductor (a conductor is anything that makes an easy path for electricity to follow) has become a standard fitting on all high buildings. Lightning rods are usually made of aluminum, which is an excellent conductor, providing a harmless path for the lightning to follow to earth.
★ *Remember that Franklin's experiment was very dangerous. Never be tempted to repeat it yourself.*

GALVANI AND VOLTA

Around 1780, Italian scientist Luigi Galvani (1737-1798) was dissecting a frog on a metal sheet. When he touched one of the dead frog's nerves with his steel scalpel, a leg twitched. Galvani experimented further and found that the frog's legs would twitch whenever they were brought into contact with two different metals, such as brass and iron. He believed that the frog's muscles were producing "animal electricity," as he called it.

Galvani sent a report of his findings to a friend, another Italian named Alessandro Volta (1745-1827). Volta repeated the experiments and decided that Galvani's explanation was wrong, reasoning that the electricity was a result of the brass and iron being in contact with each other, not by the animal tissue. Galvani was furious at being contradicted, and a bitter fight broke out between the two men.

NAMES THAT LIVE TODAY

The principles of Volta's pile allowed the development of the batteries we use today (see page 30). Volta, shown above, likened the steady flow of electricity from his pile to the flow of a river, calling it a current. The unit of electrical force that moves this current is called a volt.

Galvani's name also lives on today. The electric current set up by two metals in contact with each other is known as galvanic electricity. Iron, a metal that corrodes quickly in damp conditions, can be protected from rusting by coating it with zinc. This process is called galvanizing.

◄ Galvani experimented for many years in his laboratory. This is a picture of a print made at the time.

▲▶ Sizes of voltaic piles varied according to the output required, the biggest consisting of several hundred cells connected in a circuit. The principle is the same, whatever the size. By a chemical reaction, the copper takes up electrons from the salt solution and the zinc loses electrons to the solution. The resulting flow of electrons can be harnessed as an electric current.

1. Copper disk
2. Pasteboard disk soaked in salt water
3. Zinc disk

In 1800 Volta built a device – the voltaic pile – that proved electricity could be produced by a reaction between two different metals. The basic unit of his pile was a cell made up of a sandwich of copper, pasteboard, and zinc disks. The pasteboard was soaked in salt water. Volta built a pile of 30 to 40 three-disk cells, to form the first battery. When connected, the voltaic pile produced a steady flow of electricity. This was a breakthrough discovery, since the Leyden jar released its charge in a single surge.

The invention brought Volta fame and honor. The French emperor Napoleon Bonaparte summoned Volta for a demonstration, and fellow scientists honored the achievement. The force that moves an electric current, the volt, was named after him.

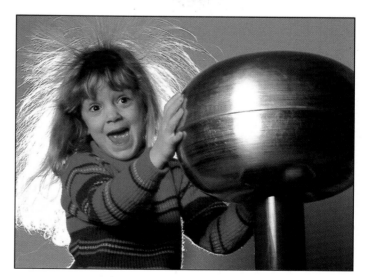

▲ In the early days of electrical research, people were fascinated by the new force, and many paid to get an electric shock. A popular demonstration involved suspending a boy with silk cords, which acted as insulators, then charging him with static electricity so that his hair stood on end. Here, a girl of today performs a similar experiment.

LIVING ELECTRICITY

Although Galvani's idea of animal electricity was rejected by Volta, it wasn't entirely wrong. When placed between two different metals, the chemicals in the body help create a very weak electrical impulse, acting like the salt solution in the pasteboard disks of the voltaic pile. When Galvani attempted to charge living tissue from a Leyden jar, the liquids acted as conductors.

The human body is a complex electrical system. The information received through the five senses – those of sight, sound, touch, taste, and smell – is passed along nerve fibers as tiny electrical signals to the brain, which is also an electrical activity center. These electrical signals are measured in tiny amounts. They travel as messengers and controllers throughout the body, especially in the brain, muscles, and sense organs. In the nineteenth century, many curious "medical" machines were developed, often with no real effect other than to cause mild electric shocks and other strange sensations to patients.

However, research did lead to such important machines as the electrocardiograph machine, or EKG(short for the German *Elektrokardiogramm*). Developed in 1900 by Willem Einthoven, the EKG detects the tiny electrical signals generated by the heart muscle. The rhythm can be shown as a moving blip on a small screen. This can then be used to monitor the progress of a hospital patient with heart trouble. Likewise, brain waves can be detected by a similar machine, the electroencephalograph, or EEG.

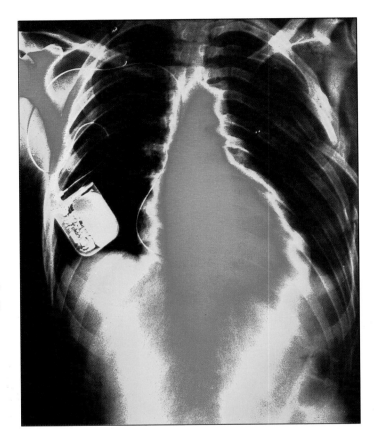

▲ The heart's pumping rhythm is an electrical process controlled by a patch of special tissue. If this tissue becomes faulty, a heart pacemaker (invented in 1960), like the one shown on the left in this X-ray picture, may be surgically implanted under the skin. This battery-powered machine, similar in size to an audio cassette, provides the regular signals that the heart needs in order to function properly.

A cross section through an electric eel's body reveals swim muscles (1), spine (2), and electric organs (3) that can build up a charge of 600 volts or more.

▲ This clock works on the same principle as Volta's pile. Acid in the fruit juice acts as an electrolyte connecting electrodes made of different metals.

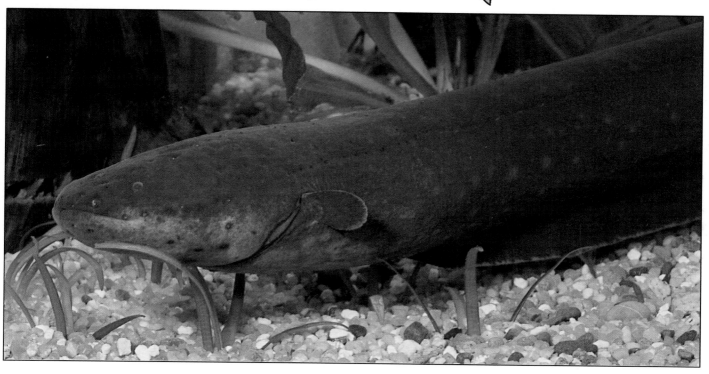

Many creatures in the animal kingdom are well known for using electricity. Electric eels and rays have special muscles that behave like living batteries. These produce pulses of electricity that can discharge through the water to shock victims. Sharks too, use electricity for homing in on their prey. About a thousand sensors in a shark's skin enable it to detect the minute electrical forces generated by the muscles of nearby fish. The result is that a hungry shark can move in with deadly accuracy, even in total darkness.

▲ Hundreds of cells in an electric eel's skin act as tiny batteries. They can deliver a massive electrical charge that is enough to stun or kill nearby prey.

◉ ELECTROCHEMISTRY

▲ Part of Volta's letter to the Royal Society in London.

Volta wrote to a famous scientific group, the Royal Society of London, to tell them about his invention. One of the members was William Nicholson (1753-1815), an English chemist, who built his own voltaic pile. He placed the ends of the battery wires in water and found that bubbles of gas were given off. The electric current was splitting the water into its two basic elements, hydrogen and oxygen. Volta had shown that a chemical reaction could cause an electric current, and now Nicholson showed that an electric current could cause a chemical reaction.

Sir Humphry Davy (1778-1829), another English chemist, carried out further experiments. He built a battery with more than 250 cells, the most powerful yet assembled. In October 1807, Davy applied the current from his new battery to molten potash. The result was astonishing. The electric current caused a chemical reaction in the potash, and drops of a silver-white metal appeared, a pure element that Davy called potassium. Within a week, using a still larger current, he extracted pure sodium from soda, and the following year he went on to discover four more new metals.

◀ Davy used a huge battery of cells for his electrolysis experiments.

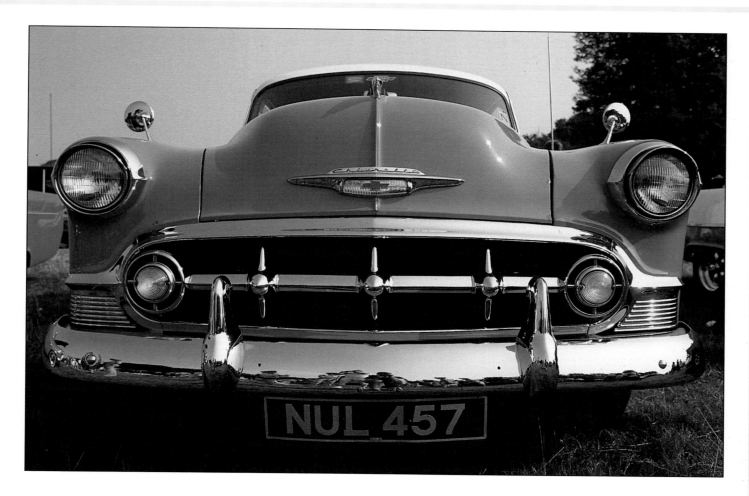

Davy gave regular lectures at the Royal Institution, founded in 1799 in London. The lectures were generally well illustrated by experiments, a tradition carried on today. Several of Davy's lectures were attended by Michael Faraday (1791-1867), who applied for a job as Davy's assistant. Faraday, perhaps more than any other man, was to carry out researches that would ultimately electrify the world, as we shall see later in this book. Continuing Davy's work in electrochemistry, Faraday gave the name electrolysis to the process of separating out elements. He called the substance to be split an electrolyte and the metal rods between which the current flowed electrodes. The positive electrode was the anode, the negative electrode the cathode, terms still used today.

▲ Electrolysis is used for many industrial processes, including plating parts of automobiles, such as the bumpers and window moldings, with chromium.

 A LABORATORY METAL

Some substances, such as potassium, can be produced only in the laboratory. In nature potassium is always found combined with other substances as a compound. When separated out by the process of electrolysis, potassium appears as a silvery metal and is soft enough to cut with a knife.

Davy's and Faraday's work led to the industrial process of electroplating. This process covers a conducting object with a thin coat of pure metal. Silver-plated cutlery is an example: silver spoons are expensive; spoons plated with silver look nice and shiny, but cost a small fraction of solid silver.

ELECTRICITY AND MAGNETISM

By the nineteenth century, much progress had been made in the understanding of electricity. For some time scientists had suspected that there was a link between electricity and magnetism, but they couldn't find it. In 1820 Danish scientist Hans Christian Oersted (1777-1851), professor of physics at Denmark's Copenhagen University, found that the needle on a compass moved when it was brought near a wire carrying an electric current. The discovery made him famous and he was invited to visit a number of science academies across Europe. During his travels he met fellow scientists Davy and Faraday.

▲ Hans Christian Oersted

▶ Oersted's equipment consisted of a battery (1), a current-carrying wire (2), and a compass (3). When the compass was moved near the wire, the needle swung away from its north-south direction (4).

Shortly after Oersted's announcement, Frenchman André-Marie Ampère (1775-1836) discovered that the movement of the compass needle followed a definite direction. If a person were to hold a wire through which current was passing with his right hand, with his thumb pointing in the direction of the current, the north pole of a magnet would always be deflected in the direction of his curling fingers. Ampère also showed that a wire coiled like a spring behaved like a bar magnet when a current was passed through it. He called this coiled wire a solenoid.

In 1823, following Ampère's descriptions, English physicist William Sturgeon (1783-1850) invented the first electromagnet. His horseshoe-shaped iron bar, surrounded by an insulated wire coil, could lift no less than twenty times its own weight as long as a current was passing through the wire.

▲ This electromagnet is used in a scrap yard for lifting heavy metal parts. It helps separate the pieces containing iron from the rest.

 AMPS

Ampère founded the science of electric currents, which he called electrodynamics. The study of stationary electric charges, on which von Guericke and Franklin had worked, he called electrostatics. The unit that measures the quantity of an electric current passing a point in a given time is called the ampere, or amp.

TELEGRAPH AND RELAY

In America, physicist Joseph Henry (1797-1878) had heard of Sturgeon's work with electromagnets. After experimenting, Henry realized that the more coils of wire there were around the iron core, the more powerful the electromagnet would be. By 1831 he had made an electromagnet that could lift over 650 pounds.

Of course, electromagnets did not have to be so powerful, and Henry put one to a much more delicate use. He made a switch that consisted of a mile-long wire with a tiny electromagnet at one end and a battery at the other. When the current was switched on, the electromagnet attracted a small iron bar, which sounded a bell. When the current was switched off, a spring pulled the iron bar back to its original position. With this device, Henry had invented the first practical system of sending simple signals electrically, the telegraph. The bell's on-off sound could be used as a signal code for sending messages.

▲ Joseph Henry worked on electromagnets, electric motors, and the electric telegraph.

◀ One of England's first telegraph lines ran between Windsor and London.

 ## RESISTANCE

All conductors resist the flow of electricity to some degree. The difference depends on the material used, its width and length, and the amount of current flow. For a given amount of current, a short, wide conductor has less resistance than a long, thin one. Georg Ohm summed up the effects in his Ohm's Law, and the unit of resistance, the ohm, is named after him.

◄ A telegraphic receiver based on a design by the German Siemens Company. Its parts included a key (1) to wind a clockwork motor for the tape. A small reservoir carried ink for the printer. Another key (2) was used for tapping out messages. Other features included terminal connections (3) and a pair of electromagnets (4).

Henry's telegraph was limited to fairly short distances. In 1826, German physicist Georg Ohm (1789-1854) had shown that different materials opposed, or resisted, the flow of an electric current to varying degrees. Materials that conducted electricity had a low resistance, but this resistance increased as the length of the conductor increased. In order to keep the same amount of current flowing, the voltage had to be increased. The resourceful Henry found a way to get around this difficulty with his electrical relay of 1835. A current just strong enough to switch on an electromagnet could be sent down a wire. The electromagnet closed a switch that turned on a second battery. The current from this battery then traveled along a further length of wire to another relay, where the operation was repeated. As many relays as were necessary could be set up to cover great distances, and because the length of each stage was short, the voltage needed remained low.

Henry did not patent the relay because he believed that scientific discoveries should be freely available for everyone. When Henry met Samuel Morse he was happy to explain how the relay worked. Morse obtained a patent for the electric telegraph in 1840 and the first telegraph line was opened in 1844, between Baltimore and Washington, DC.

☀ SENDING MESSAGES

Morse never admitted how much he learned from Henry. The Morse code became the most widely used message system ever. As the railroads were being built across the United States, so telegraph wires were strung beside the tracks. This way, apart from other messages, timetable changes or train delays could be flashed between telegraph stations along the route. When radio was invented, Morse code was put to use as a simple way of transmitting messages. The best known part of the Morse code is the message SOS (... – – – ...), still used today. The letters were chosen as a help signal because they are easy to understand.

THE ELECTRIC MOTOR

Oersted's discovery that electricity and magnetism were related led to another important invention. In 1821, the year after Oersted announced his findings, Michael Faraday observed that the force that acted between a magnet and a wire carrying an electric current moved the magnet in a circle around the wire.

Faraday performed experiments that arranged magnets and wires in such a way that either the magnets or the wires were free to rotate. When a current was passed through the free-moving wire it would turn around the fixed magnet, or the free-moving magnet would turn around the fixed wire. Faraday's spinning wires and magnets were little more than toys, but this was the first time that electrical energy had been converted into mechanical energy. It was the first stage in the development of the electric motor.

It was almost ten years later, in 1830, that Joseph Henry used electromagnets to make the first electric motor that could do useful work. By 1840 electric motors, running on expensive batteries, were being used for machines such as drills and lathes.

▲ This picture shows one of Faraday's machines. He called it an "electro-magnetic rotation apparatus." On the left, a magnet is going around a fixed wire; on the right a wire is spinning around a magnet.

▶ **This diagram shows the basic layout of a simple electric motor.**
1. **Current flows through a coil of wire, called the armature.**
2. **The magnetic force pushes one side up and the other side down.**
3. **Mounting the armature on a shaft allows it to spin around.**

MOTORS BY THE MILLIONS

Life today would be unthinkable without the myriad electric motors, large and small, that perform a multitude of jobs. In a typical three-bedroom house, there are three dozen or more motors whirring away, running everything from microwave ovens and electric clocks to exhaust fans and compact disc players. In a luxury car, the motor count runs high, too – even doors are sometimes powered.

▲ Early subway systems were natural uses for clean electric power.

▲ A lineup of just some of the electric gadgets that are used in today's homes.

THE GENERATOR

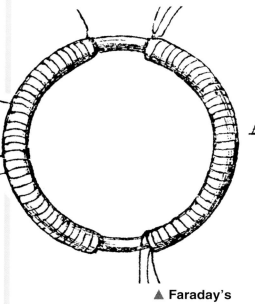

▲ **Faraday's induction ring was two coils of wire around a soft iron core. They were kept apart by calico fabric and tied in place with string.**

A The electric motor produces movement from electricity; the generator produces electricity from movement. The first generator was developed by Michael Faraday in 1831 during the course of a series of experiments.

Faraday wound two separate coils of wire around an iron ring. He linked the first wire to a galvanometer, an instrument for measuring electric current. The second wire was connected to a battery. The wires were carefully insulated so that they had no contact with each other, yet when the current in the second wire was switched on and off the galvanometer registered a current in the first wire. This was caused, or induced, by the variation in the magnetic field produced by current in the second wire.

Faraday thought – correctly – that magnetic lines of force extended out when an electrical current was flowing and collapsed in again when it was switched off. The lines of force cutting across the second wire induced the electric current.

▲ **Faraday's electric generator was a copper disk that spun between the poles of a horseshoe magnet.**

The discovery of this phenomenon – electromagnetic induction – was crucial. Faraday went on to demonstrate that an electric current was also produced when a coil was moved near a magnet or a magnet moved near a coil. In a classic experiment, Faraday placed a copper disk, which could be rotated using a crank, between the poles of a horseshoe magnet. One contact wire trailed against the shaft running through the disk and a second wire trailed against the disk itself. Both wires were linked to a galvanometer. When the disk was turned through the magnet's lines of force the galvanometer registered a flow of current. With this device, Faraday turned mechanical energy into electricity and perfected the first generator. By the 1860s, electricity generators were in widespread use. These large generators used electromagnets and were driven by steam engines. Improvements in generator design made it possible to produce electricity on a huge scale.

▲ Michael Faraday, shown here lecturing at the Royal Society, was largely a self-taught experimenter and one of the greatest electrical pioneers. He is probably best remembered for the generator, but his discoveries ranged across the fields of chemistry and magnetism, too.

◀ The generating equipment in a modern power plant.

 ## GENERATING POWER

Generators are the foundation of modern life. Without them, power plants (see page 28) would not be able to produce the massive amounts of electricity needed to run homes, offices, and factories. The source of energy used to turn such generators varies widely. The range includes natural resources such as coal, oil, gas, wind and water power, and nuclear energy.

LIGHTING UP THE WORLD

The familiar lightbulb we use today was not developed until 1878. Before then, the carbon-arc lamp was the nearest thing to a practical electric light. The carbon lamp was an 1808 invention that used a pair of close-set carbon rods with a powerful electric current passing between them. The spark that jumped across the gap produced a brilliant white light, but the rods burned away in the intense heat and had to be replaced every few hours. Many improvements were made to carbon-arc lights – their bright output was especially useful in lighthouses – but the incandescent system was the type that evolved into the lightbulbs we know today.

▲ Early lightbulbs from the Edison Company. These used carbon thread filaments, which lasted much longer than the fine cotton that was used in Edison's first bulb.

▼ The secrets of a lightbulb revealed. The bright glow is caused by the high resistance of a very long and very thin wire. The bulb is not very efficient, however, because much energy is wasted as heat.

The first incandescent bulbs (the name means "glowing with intense heat") were developed independently by Sir Joseph Swan (1828-1914) in England and Thomas Alva Edison (1847-1931) in the United States. The key to success was to put the filament – the thin wire that glowed – in a near vacuum. This kept it from burning away too quickly. Swan was first to demonstrate a practical bulb, in December 1878. When Edison – perhaps the most prolific inventor ever known – announced earlier the same year that he would try to find a longer-lasting bulb, the value of shares in U.S. companies supplying gas for lighting fell at once, because people had such confidence in Edison's abilities.

1. **Coiled-coil filament packs more wire in the bulb for more light output. Tungsten is the most commonly used material today, because it has a very high melting point.**
2. **Glass bulb**
3. **Fine wire frame supports the filament.**
4. **Bulb filled with argon gas, which prevents the filament from burning away.**

In October 1879, after more than a year's work and thousands of experiments, Edison produced his first electric lightbulb. Four years later, he and Swan teamed up and went into business as the Edison and Swan United Electric Light Company. By the 1890s whole cities were lit by electricity and four million bulbs a year were coming off the production lines. At the same time, vast improvements in design were made – an early bulb lasted 45 hours or so; by 1900, 500 hours was not uncommon. Today, the average lightbulb can last thousands of hours.

Gas-discharge lamps were first developed in 1909 by Frenchman Georges Claude. He used a tube containing neon gas, which glowed when an electric current was discharged through it. The bright light uses little current and remains cool, wasting little energy as heat, unlike incandescent bulbs. Such gas-discharge lamps are widely used for advertising, because the tubes can be bent into all sorts of shapes. Different gases are mixed with neon to produce different colors. Street lighting often uses sodium vapor, which gives a yellow, fog-piercing light, or mercury vapor, which gives a hard blue-white light.

The latest energy-saving bulbs are coated inside with a material that glows. They are more expensive to buy than traditional incandescent bulbs, but they last much longer and are cheaper to run.

▲ **Millions of lightbulbs illuminate the skyline of this city.**

 FAREWELL TO DARKNESS

Electric lighting has been a real world changer. Apart from simple things, like being able to read and write comfortably whatever the time of day or night, electric lighting has helped to make the world a safer place. Imagine cars and trucks without powerful headlights or city streets without powerful overhead lighting systems.

ELECTRICITY FOR ALL

The electric light, and the other electric appliances that followed, needed a reliable source of electricity if they were to be of much use. That meant efficient generators and a means of supplying the electricity to the consumers.

Edison's first power plant was built on Pearl Street, New York City, in 1882. It consisted of three generators that supplied electricity to 225 houses. As demand for electricity increased – for ovens and heaters in homes and electric motors in workshops and factories – so the efficiency of power plants and distribution networks had to be improved. Ohm's law set a limit on the ability of cables to carry electric current – it was impossible to extend the cables over more than a few miles.

The solution to the problem was two-fold: alternating current and the transformer. Up to this point power had been supplied by direct current, in which the charge flows in just one direction. In 1887, Nikola Tesla (1856-1943), a former employee of Edison, patented a generating system that used alternating current in which the current flow reverses direction about 50 times a second. It makes no difference to an electrical device which way the current is flowing; it will work as long as there is movement of electrons.

▲ Electricity from a battery flows in one direction and is called direct current. Electricity from a power plant is called alternating current – electrons move back and forth in a wire instead of in one direction.
1. Power plant generators have coils like that of an electric motor. As a coil is turned between two magnets, current is made.
2. The amount of current varies as the coil rotates, from two peaks of current to none at all, in a rapid on-off flow of 50 two-way cycles per second.

▶ An early power plant. Most were fueled with coal hauled by train or barge. Power plants were, and still are, built near convenient fuel supplies.

An alternating current produces a magnetic field that switches on and off rapidly. A transformer can change the voltage of an alternating current. The current flows into a coil wound around the iron core of the transformer. By the process of electromagnetic induction, current is induced in a second coil (Michael Faraday's double-coil device of 1831 was actually the first transformer). The voltage of the induced current depends on the ratio of the turns of the coils. If the second coil has five times as many turns as the first, the voltage goes up five times. Similarly, if there are fewer turns in the second coil the voltage is reduced.

The beauty of the system is that by using alternating current, voltage can be stepped up at power plants for transmission along cables, then stepped down again for use in homes. Electricity could now be distributed over long distances.

▲ One of the more serious aspects of power generation is pollution. Unless proper cleaning equipment is installed, a coal-fired plant will create acid rain, affecting life downwind. Even waste steam from the cooling towers can cause local weather changes. With nuclear power plants, the safe disposal of dangerous waste will be a concern for centuries to come.

⚙ PORTABLE POWER

Power from the electric company is convenient for permanent electrical equipment such as ovens, refrigerators, and lighting. For people on the move, however, it is essential to have a portable power source.

The most familiar way of powering gadgets such as flashlights and portable stereos is by using the familiar tube-shaped dry cell. The dry cell is based on a design invented in 1865 by a French engineer named Georges Leclanché (1839-82). It consists of a zinc case and a central carbon rod, which are the electrodes, separated by an ammonium chloride paste, which acts as the electrolyte. The paste is used instead of liquid to make the cell spill-proof. If two or more dry cells are used together, it is called a "battery" of cells. They are linked in the same way as the cells in Volta's pile of 1799. Today, we think of a dry cell as a battery, whether we use one or several.

▲ Video cameras use rechargeable batteries, typically nickel-cadmium types.

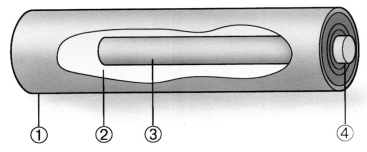

The first rechargeable battery was invented by French physicist Gaston Planté in 1859. It was similar in design to the liquid batteries that are used today in cars. A series of lead and lead oxide plates are immersed in an electrolyte solution of sulfuric acid and water. A chemical reaction between the acid and the lead plates, in which the plates are converted to lead sulfate, causes current to flow, supplying electricity for starting the motor. Once a car is started, a type of generator called an alternator recharges the battery by applying current to the plates. The plates are converted back to lead and lead oxide ready for reuse. Such batteries are good for about three years.

▲ This type of dry cell is typical of the sort used in small appliances. Various materials can be used. Mercury is common in small hearing-aid type cells.
1. Zinc case
2. Chemical paste
3. Carbon rod
4. Brass end cap

Rechargeable nickel-cadmium dry cells were used industrially as early as 1909. Improvements in recent years have made them suitable for home use as well, and they are used in anything that needs truly portable power, from video cameras to cordless screwdrivers.

With pollution from gasoline-fueled cars a major issue, companies in Europe, Japan, and the United States are developing electric cars powered by advanced batteries. They are not perfect yet though – a typical performance is that of the GM Impact, which can hit a top speed of 100 mph but is limited to a 150-mile range before needing to be recharged.

Another source of portable power is the fuel cell, invented in 1959. It converts chemical energy directly into electrical energy. In the most common type, hydrogen and oxygen gases are used as fuels, with hot potassium hydroxide as the electrolyte. As long as there is a continuous flow of the two fuels, the cell provides electricity with pure water as a by-product, making it ideal for use in manned spacecraft.

▲ The space shuttle *Orbiter* uses three fuel cells for electricity while in space. They supply about the same amount of power that is used by 24 houses back on Earth. The wastewater produced by the fuel cells is used by the astronauts for drinking, cooking, and washing.

ELECTROMAGNETIC WAVES

▲ James Clerk Maxwell wrote his first scientific paper at fifteen, when he was still in school. His theories of electromagnetism form the basis of much of our present knowledge.

James Clerk Maxwell (1831-79) was a Scottish mathematician and physicist who linked the findings of Oersted, Faraday, and other scientists into a group of equations that summarized all that was known about electricity and magnetism. Maxwell showed that they did not exist apart but were bound together. A magnetic field moving back and forth, or oscillating, gives rise to an oscillating electric field, which in turn produces a magnetic field, and so on. The fields keep in step with each other as an electromagnetic "wave," moving outward from a source at the speed of light, 186,282 miles per second.

It was not until the 1880s, after Maxwell's death, that German physicist Heinrich Hertz (1857-94) proved that Maxwell's wave theory was right. In one of Hertz's early experiments he used a pair of high-voltage coils with a gap between them. When the power was switched on, a spark leaped across the gap, the rapidly oscillating electric current in it producing an electromagnetic wave. As a receiver, Hertz used a pair of rods with a gap between them. When the waves were picked up, a spark crackled between the rods. For some time these waves were called Hertzian waves, but after they were put to practical use by the Italian Guglielmo Marconi for transmitting messages, they became known by the name we use today – radio waves.

▶ The electromagnetic spectrum is the name given to the range of different types of radiation. The part of the spectrum that our eyes can detect is called visible light. We can feel infrared as heat, and too much ultraviolet causes sunburn and skin cancer. Microwaves are used in domestic ovens, radar equipment, and communications. X rays are used in medicine to take pictures of the inside of the body, showing bones and body tissues beneath the skin.

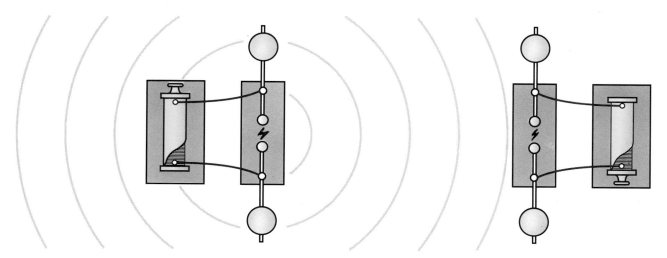

▲ The experimental apparatus of Heinrich Hertz generated a powerful electric spark. As this spark jumped the gap between two rods, it created a burst of radio waves that moved outward, like ripples in water when a stone is thrown in. The receiving apparatus picked up the radio signals, which in turn created a smaller and weaker spark.

 # PIONEER OF THE RADIO AGE

From Hertz's pioneering work, the radio has gone on to conquer the world of communications. Guglielmo Marconi developed Hertz's basic ideas, first in Bologna, Italy, then later in Great Britain. Marconi had wireless telegraphy equipment working reliably by the 1890s. This was a halfway stage to today's radio – messages were sent using Morse code, but without the wires of a conventional telegraph setup. By 1901 Marconi was sending messages across the Atlantic Ocean, and, before long, regular broadcasts of news and entertainment were filling the air waves. By the 1930s, a radio in the home was common, and families sat around the radio to listen to broadcasts in much the same way they would later watch television programs.

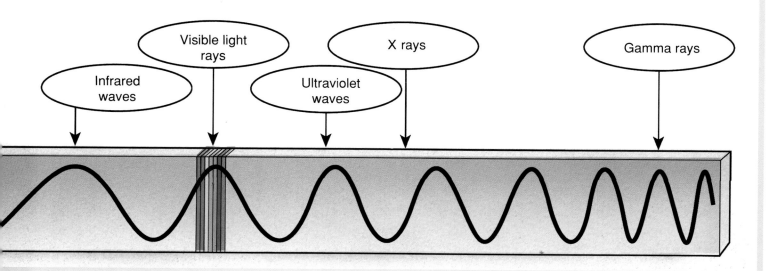

☀ THE CATHODE-RAY TUBE

In the 1850s, German scientist Julius Plücker (1801-68) noticed a mysterious green glow surrounding the cathode in a vacuum tube with which he was experimenting. Plücker was not the first to have spotted this – in 1838, Michael Faraday had noticed the effect, but the vacuum tubes at the time were not good enough to investigate further. As vacuum tubes improved, researchers found that the glow was in fact a stream of rays. In experiments with these cathode rays, British scientist William Crookes (1832-1919) put a small metal cross inside a vacuum tube. When the power was switched on, the end of the tube glowed green where the cathode rays hit it, while in the middle the metal cross cast a shadow, proving that the rays moved in straight lines. Experiments showed that they could be bent, or deflected, by magnets placed nearby.

▲ William Crookes perfected his cathode-ray tube in 1880.

▶ Crookes used a glass tube with a cathode, spraying out a stream of electrons past a tin cross at one end. A shadow was cast by the cross at the far end of the tube
1. Glass tube
2. Cathode
3. Anode
4. Maltese cross
5. Shadow cast by cross

Another British researcher, Joseph John Thomson (1856-1940), knew that cathode rays could be bent by a magnetic field; he carried out experiments that proved the rays were negatively charged. In 1881, he discovered that the rays were made of particles that were far lighter than even the lightest atom, hydrogen. This was a breakthrough – until this time, people had thought the atom was a single unit that could not be split.

Thomson's research showed that, in fact, the atom had to be made up of smaller components. At first, Thomson called these particles "corpuscles," but eventually they were called electrons. This was a word that was used some years earlier by the Irish physicist George Stoney, after the original Greek word for amber.

☀ ELECTRONIC DISPLAYS

From the research done on cathode rays has come our present knowledge of the atom and its structure. The cathode-ray tube itself, now usually shortened to CRT, has been developed into the familiar picture tube used in television sets, radar screens, computer monitors, and all the other electronic displays that are used every day across the world.

THE ELECTRONIC AGE

Electronics, the study of devices that rely on the controlled flow of electrons, dates from 1904, with the invention of the diode valve, or electron tube, by British electrical engineer Sir John Fleming (1849-1945). It turned on when current flowed in one direction and off when the flow went the other way. Valves, with their one-way current flow, made it possible to build radios that could receive weak broadcast signals. Two years later, the American Lee De Forest (1873-1961) developed the idea by making a valve that could increase, or amplify, current as well. De Forest's improved design, the triode valve, led to the use of loudspeakers for listening to a radio instead of headphones.

Over the next thirty years valves were put to many other uses, such as in the first televisions and computers. They were bulky and fragile, however, and people looked for something smaller and tougher that could do the same job. In 1947, a three-man team led by William Shockley at the U.S. Bell Telephone Laboratories invented the transistor.

▲ This early computer dwarfs today's equipment. Despite this, an average modern desktop machine is much more powerful.

▶ Key stages in the development of electronic components included delicate glass valves, which came in many shapes and sizes. A transistor (far right) does the job of a valve, while being much smaller and more reliable. Today's integrated circuits pack thousands of transistors on a tiny piece of silicon chip. Each stage of size reduction has improved speed, power, and reliability many times over.

▶ This close-up of an electronic circuit shows how complex such devices can be.

The main materials in a transistor are called semiconductors. For as long as electricity has been studied, it has been known that some solids will conduct electricity and some will not. However, there are elements, such as silicon and germanium, that fall somewhere in between. These elements are called semiconductors. They can be produced either with extra electrons (n-type) or so that they attract electrons (p-type). By putting p-type and n-type semiconductors together in particular ways, it is possible to make devices that can switch, amplify, or detect electric current.

The transistor had huge advantages over the old-fashioned and bulky valve – it was lighter, smaller, more reliable, and a lot cheaper to make. This meant that electronic equipment could be made much smaller, and the first transistor radios used the new technology with great success.

The next leap in the evolution of electronics came when Americans Jack Kilby and Robert Noyce developed the integrated circuit in 1958. The integrated circuit had several components on a single piece of semiconductor material. Previously, transistors had been linked individually to other components in an electrical circuit, just as valves had been. By the 1980s it was possible to have a million or more transistors on a single silicon microchip. The result has been an explosion in the use of machines that use them – from desktop and laptop computers to portable telephones and satellite navigation systems.

◀ An amplifier transistor has a p-type semiconductor with an n-type on either side. An increase in the current flowing into the base (1) causes more of an increase in the flow through the collector (2). This stronger signal can be used in various ways, such as to power stereo speakers.

☀ ELECTRONIC PARTS

Transistors are not the only semiconductor parts in an electronic circuit. Others include: resistors, which control the amount of current flowing in a circuit; diodes, which allow current to pass in one direction only; and light-emitting diodes (LEDs), which glow when current passes through them. LEDs are used for indicator lights and in some calculators. Capacitors store an electric charge, releasing it when required, such as when a camera uses an electronic flash.

ELECTRICITY FROM LIGHT

When Hertz was conducting radio-wave experiments in 1887, he noticed that the sparks produced in his detector were influenced by light falling on the spark transmitter. He saw that the effect was greatest when light fell on the transmitter's cathode, but he did not take his investigations much further.

Other scientists discovered that light was causing the cathode to give off electrons, but they had no explanation for why this should be so. An answer came from the German-born scientist Albert Einstein (1879-1955). In 1905 he proposed that light, and all other forms of electromagnetic radiation, could sometimes act as particles rather than waves. When a particle of light, called a photon, struck an electron in a solid, the electron absorbed the photon's energy. If the photon had enough energy, the electron was ejected from the solid. Einstein was saying that electromagnetic radiation could act as a wave or as a stream of particles.

▲ The photoelectric effect is at work in a solar cell or photocell, which turns light into electricity. Energy from photons (1) frees electrons (2) from a material such as silicon, and the resulting current flow can be used as a source of power. Solar cells are in wide use today, from powering calculators to supplying electricity aboard satellites.

▲ Uses for solar cells range wider every day. This Honda Dream rolled to victory in the 1993 trans-Australia World Solar Challenge race. The car averaged 52 mph over the 1,865-mile (3,000 km) course, hitting speeds of up to 70 mph. The Dream's solar cell array charged 83 silver-zinc battery cells, which in turn powered an electric motor.

Two other ways of producing electricity are through heat and pressure. Heating one junction of two conductors results in a current flow. Known as thermoelectricity, it was originally studied by German scientist Thomas Seebeck (1770-1831) in the 1820s. Piezoelectricity is that produced by pressure. Pressing some crystals, such as quartz, results in a current. Devices that use the piezoelectricity include quartz watches and the hand sparkers sometimes used to light the heating elements on gas stoves.

A SOLAR FUTURE

Solar cells don't make headline news, but they stand a good chance of being a leading power source in the future. Constantly improving technology means that weight and size are shrinking while power output goes up. It's in small ways that solar cells are creeping into our lives – whether it is a laptop computer that is freed from dependence on the electrical outlet, or the solar-powered air conditioner that keeps a car interior cool while the engine is off.

◀ **Solar cells cover the surface of this satellite. As long as the craft remains in sunlight, electricity can be generated to run all the systems.**

NEW FRONTIERS

A t room temperature, even the best conductor shows some resistance to an electric current passing through it. However, back in 1910, Dutch physicist Heike Kamerlingh Onnes (1853-1926) was researching the behavior of matter at very low temperatures. He discovered that the resistance of materials to electrons passing through them dropped off to zero at temperatures close to -270°C (-518°F). He called this astonishing property superconductivity.

As we saw earlier, one of the problems in transporting electricity from generator to user is the high voltages needed to overcome resistance in the wires and cables. If superconducting wires could be used, the cost of supplying electricity would be greatly reduced. However, in most materials superconductivity only appears at extremely low temperatures, and the expense of the cooling systems required would be far greater than any savings made.

RESEARCHING THE FUTURE

In Japan, scientists are working on a project involving quantum wires. These would be so tiny that a computer rivaling today's wardrobe-sized Cray supercomputer could be the size of a book.

Elsewhere, scientists are working on developing plastics that conduct electricity. These would revolutionize many areas – a portable radio, for example, could have its battery built into the casing.

◄ A magnet floats above a ceramic super-conductor. The vapor is from liquid nitrogen, used to keep the material cool.

The MLU-002 maglev is used for developing high-speed transportation links in Japan. In Europe, the German Transrapid magnetic hovertrain is a cutting-edge design that is ready to catapult commuter speeds to 250 mph and beyond. A 175-mile route between Berlin and Hamburg should be in operation by the year 2002. The journey will take just 53 minutes. The train relies on research into superconductivity for its advanced design.

Ever since Onnes' discovery, scientists have searched for materials that are superconducting at higher temperatures. In 1988 superconductors that worked at around -150°C (-238°F) were found. This is still very cold, but components can be cooled to this temperature with liquid nitrogen, which is not too expensive to make. Scientists are now trying to apply the technology to computers – using superconducting circuits, such computers would be hundreds of times faster than anything that is available today. And a French team claims to have discovered superconductors that will work much nearer to 0°C (32°F), which would really revolutionize electronics.

In the course of 400 years of research, scientists have established that electricity involves the movement of electrons. If an object has an accumulation of electrons, it will have an electric charge. But what moves the electron along? Physicist Richard Feynman (1918-1988) and others have proposed that electrons exchange even smaller, massless, chargeless particles to propel themselves, but really the answer is not yet known.

CHRONOLOGY OF ADVANCE

Here is a list of some of the people whose science discoveries, inventions, and improvements have brought about the world of today.

Thales of Miletus Greek philosopher (625? B.C.-547? B.C.). Considered to be the father of modern science. The first person known to have studied magnetism and the first to ask, "What is the universe made of?"

William Gilbert English doctor and scientist (1544-1603). Performed many experiments on electrical and magnetic forces. His book *De Magnete* set the scene for the scientific study of electricity and magnetism.

Otto von Guericke German physicist (1602-86). Famous for his experiments involving vacuums. Devised the first machine for generating an electric charge.

Charles du Fay French physicist (1698-1739). Studied the ways in which objects with an electric charge attract and repel one another.

Benjamin Franklin American statesman and scientist (1706-90). One of the signers of the Declaration of Independence, 1776. Proved the electrical nature of lightning by flying a kite in a thunderstorm.

Charles Coulomb French physicist (1736-1806). Inventor of instruments for measuring electric charges and the forces between magnets. The coulomb, the unit of electric charge, is named after him.

Luigi Galvani Italian anatomist (1737-98). Accidentally discovered that two metals could react together to give an electric current but did not recognize what he had found. The galvanometer, a device for detecting electric currents, is named after him.

Alessandro Volta Italian physicist (1745-1827). A friend of Galvani who correctly interpreted Galvani's findings and used this knowledge to make the first battery, the voltaic pile. The volt, the unit of electrical force, is named after him.

William Nicholson English chemist (1753-1815). Built his own voltaic pile and showed that electricity could be used to break up chemical compounds.

André-Marie Ampère French physicist and mathematician (1775-1836). Founder of the science of moving electric currents, called electrodynamics. The unit of electric current, the ampere or amp, is named after him.

Hans Christian Oersted Danish physicist (1777-1851). Discoverer of electromagnetism.

Sir Humphry Davy English chemist (1778-1829). Discovered a number of metals, including sodium and calcium, by using electrolysis to extract them from their compounds.

Sir Humphry Davy

William Sturgeon English physicist (1783-1850). Inventor of the electromagnet.

Dominique Francois-Jean Arago French physicist (1786-1853). After Oersted's discovery of electro-magnetism, showed that metals other than iron could be magnetized.

Georg Simon Ohm German physicist (1789-1854). Defined the law that showed the relationship between current, voltage, and resistance in an electric circuit. The unit of resistance, the ohm, is named after him.

Michael Faraday English chemist and physicist (1791-1867). Despite having no formal education, he became one of the greatest scientists ever known. Inventor of the electric motor, the electric generator, and the transformer and discoverer of electromagnetic induction.

Joseph Henry American physicist (1797-1878). A scientist on a par with Faraday who made many of the same discoveries independently. Inventor of the electric relay and the first practical electric motor.

Sir Joseph Swan English physicist and chemist (1828-1914). Inventor of an electric lightbulb that rivaled that invented by Thomas Edison. Swan formed a joint electric company with Edison in 1883.

James Clerk Maxwell Scottish mathematician and physicist (1831-79). First person to describe electricity and magnetism mathematically and predict the existence of electromagnetic waves. Also took the first color photograph in 1861.

Gaston Planté French physicist (1834-89). Inventor of the rechargeable battery.

Georges Leclanché French engineer (1839-82). Inventor of an electric cell that is the basis of the batteries we use today.

Thomas Alva Edison American inventor (1847-1931). A prolific inventor who took out over 1,000 patents. Invented the first practical electric lightbulb and the phonograph and showed the first moving pictures on a strip of film.

Sir John Ambrose Fleming English electrical engineer (1849-1945). Inventor of the valve for controlling the flow of electric current.

Nikola Tesla Croatian-American engineer (1856-1943). Inventor of the alternating current system by which electricity is sent efficiently from power plant to consumer.

Sir Joseph John Thomson English physicist (1856-1940). Discoverer of the electron. Electrons are present in all atoms and are the fundamental units of electric charge. When asked what one looked like he replied, "It's a red-nosed pixie chasing other pixies around."

Heinrich Hertz German physicist (1857-94). Discoverer of radio waves. The unit of wave frequency or cycle, the hertz (Hz), is named after him. One hertz equals one cycle per second.

Lee De Forest American inventor (1873-1961). Improved Fleming's valve, enabling it to amplify current as well as direct it. Also demonstrated the first moving pictures with sound in 1923.

Heinrich Hertz

Guglielmo Marconi Italian scientist (1874-1937). Developed early radio broadcasting, the first long-distance communications system that did not require wires.

Albert Einstein German-American physicist (1879-1955). More than anyone else, Albert Einstein's ideas have shaped physics in the twentieth century. His discovery of the photoelectric effect and his theories of relativity changed forever the way we believe the universe works. By showing that mass and energy were interchangeable, he pointed the way toward harnessing the power of the atom.

William Shockley English-American physicist (1910-89). Led the team of scientists that invented the transistor, opening the way for compact electronic devices.

GLOSSARY

Alternating current An electric current that reverses its direction again and again, very rapidly. Often abbreviated AC.

Amber A yellowish substance that is the fossil form of the resin that oozes from some trees. Amber acquires an electric charge when rubbed. The word *electricity* comes from the Greek word for amber, *elektron.*

Ampere The unit of electric current; it measures the rate of flow of an electric charge. Usually shortened to amp.

Battery Two or more electrical cells in a series. A battery stores chemical energy, which can be converted into electrical energy.

Catalyst A substance that changes the rate of a chemical reaction without being changed itself.

Cathode rays Streams of electrons from the cathode in a vacuum tube.

Cell A unit for producing electricity in which two electrodes are in contact with an electrolyte. Chemical reactions between the electrodes and the electrolyte produce an electric current.

Compound A substance that consists of atoms of more than one element.

Direct current An electric current that always flows in the same direction, such as that which comes from a battery. It is often abbreviated DC.

Dry cell A cell in which the electrolyte is in paste form. The batteries commonly used in radios, calculators, and other portable gadgets are dry cells.

Electric charge A property that gives rise to electrical and magnetic effects; it may be positive or negative. Like charges repel, opposite charges attract.

Electric current The flow of electrons through a conductor. It may also be used to mean the rate at which an electric charge flows past a point (*see* ampere).

Electrode One of the two parts of an electrical circuit that are in contact with the solution during electrolysis. The positive electrode is called the anode, the negative electrode the cathode.

◀ **This cutaway diagram shows one form of a Leyden jar. It consists of a glass jar with tin foil coatings, inside and outside, on which an electric charge can be stored. A brass rod contacts the inner foil to transfer a charge into the jar. The charge can then be stored until the brass rod is connected to a conductor. A rubber stopper prevents the rod from touching the neck of the jar.**

Electrodynamics The science of moving electric currents.

Electrolysis A process by which a compound is broken down into its elements by passing an electric current through it.

Electrolyte A substance that increases the ability of a liquid to conduct electricity when the electrolyte is dissolved in it.

Electromagnet A magnet consisting of a soft iron core around which a coil of insulated wire is wound. When a current is passed through the wire the core becomes magnetized.

Electromagnetic induction
Production of an electric current in a conductor by a changing magnetic field.

Electromagnetic wave Radiation consisting of electric and magnetic fields moving together at right angles to one another. Electromagnetic waves travel at the speed of light, about 186,282 miles per second. Radio waves, visible light, and X rays are all examples of electromagnetic waves.

Electron A tiny, negatively charged particle that forms part of every atom. Electrons move in orbits around an atom's central nucleus. Free electrons flow in a current.

Electrostatics The study of electric charges that are at rest and the forces that act between them.

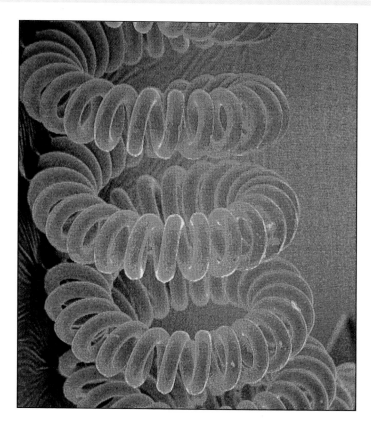

◀ **A very close look at a lightbulb filament. The tight coils enable more filament to be packed into a given length, allowing a brighter light.**

Filament The thin wire inside a lightbulb that glows when a current is passed through it. Filaments are usually made of the metal tungsten because of its high heat resistance – tungsten can reach 6,250°F (3,400°C) before it melts.

Fuel cell A cell in which chemical energy is converted into electrical energy. In the simplest type, hydrogen is combined with oxygen to form water, releasing electrons in the process to produce an electric current. Used aboard the space shuttle *Orbiter*.

Galvanic electricity A steady flow of electric current.

Galvanometer An instrument for detecting and measuring small electric currents.

Generator A device that changes movement energy into electrical energy.

Insulator A substance that is a poor conductor of electricity and stops it from flowing. Typical examples are rubber and most plastics.

Integrated circuit A miniature electronic circuit produced on the surface of a single semiconductor, such as silicon. These circuits are widely used in electronic equipment such as computers and calculators.

Leyden jar Device for storing an electric charge, invented in 1745.

Lines of force Imaginary lines in a magnetic or electric field that allow us to picture the strength and direction of the field.

Lodestone A kind of magnetite. Magnetite is a highly magnetic form of the metallic ore iron oxide. Lodestones were used as compasses by early sailors and explorers.

Magnetic field The field of force associated with the magnetism of a magnetic object. The magnitude and direction of the force can be measured at each point in the field.

Magnetic poles The parts of a magnet from which the magnetic force seems to come. One is the north pole and the other the south pole. Like poles repel each other and opposites attract.

Magnetism The name given to the effects associated with a magnetic field. A magnetic field is produced by magnetic materials and whenever an electric current flows.

Microchip Sometimes shortened simply to *chip*, a single crystal of a semiconductor that can carry out many functions in an electronic circuit.

Photon A particle of electromagnetic radiation. Photons are involved in all electromagnetic interactions.

Potash A name given to any of a number of compounds containing the element potassium.

Relay A device in which the current in one electrical circuit is controlled by changing the current in another.

Resinous electricity A type of "electrical fluid" thought to exist by Charles du Fay. The other type was vitreous electricity.

Resistance A measurement of a material's opposition to the flow of an electric charge through it. Measured in ohms.

Semiconductor A material that has a resistance to electrical current somewhere between that of a conductor and an insulator.

Soda A name given to any of a number of compounds containing sodium.

Solar cell An electric cell that produces electricity from the energy in light.

Solenoid A coil of wire that generates a magnetic field when an electric current is passed through it.

Static electricity The effects produced by electric charges that are at rest and the forces that act between objects that have an electric charge.

Sulfur A chemical element found around volcanoes. At one time people believed that the earth was largely made of sulfur.

◀ **Earth's magnetic field extends from the poles, like that of a bar magnet.**

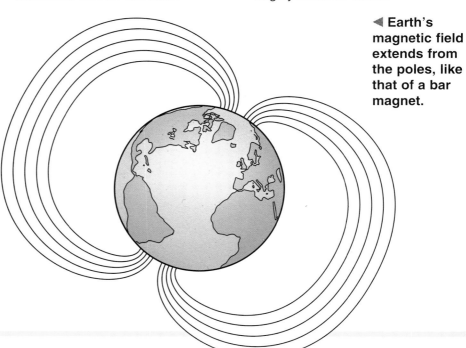

Superconductivity Absence of resistance to an electric current. Occurs in some substances at very low temperatures.

Telegraph Device for sending messages long distances. It uses an electric current that passes along a wire linking a transmitter and receiver.

◀ **A calculator, with its micro-electronic insides revealed.**

Transformer A device that transfers electrical energy from one alternating current to another, changing voltage or current in the process.

Transistor Tiny device made from semiconductor material that can act as a switch or amplifier in an electric circuit. Transistors are the basic components of electronic equipment. They were first invented in 1948 by an American team headed by William Shockley.

Vacuum tube Electronic component, such as a valve or cathode-ray tube, that has had the air extracted from the interior.

Valve Device for controlling the flow of electricity in an electrical circuit. Valves have now been almost universally replaced by transistors, which are smaller, cheaper, and more reliable. An exception is some top-quality stereo equipment. Valves, say the makers, give a

sound that seems more musical to the ears of serious music lovers.

Volt The measure of electrical energy at a particular point. A positive charge moves from a point with high voltage to one with low voltage.

Voltaic pile A form of battery invented by Alessandro Volta in which cells were joined together to produce an electric current.

 # FURTHER READING

Brophy, Michael. *Michael Faraday.* Pioneers of Science. New York: Bookwright Press, 1991.

Catherall, Ed. *Exploring Electricity.* Exploring Science. Milwaukee: Raintree Steck-Vaughn, 1990.

Feldman, Eve B. *Benjamin Franklin: Scientist and Inventor.* First Books. New York: Franklin Watts, 1990.

Hooper, Tony. *Electricity.* Breakthrough. Milwaukee: Raintree Steck-Vaughn, 1993.

Ireland, Karin. *Albert Einstein.* Pioneers in Change. Mahwah, NJ: Silver Burdett, 1989.

Kerrod, Robin. *Energy Resources.* World's Resources. New York: Thomson Learning, 1994.

Lafferty, Peter. *The Inventor Through History.* Journey Through History. New York: Thomson Learning, 1993.

Lampton, Christopher. *Thomas Alva Edison.* North Bellmore, NY: Marshall Cavendish Corp., 1991.

Leon, George deLucenay. *Electronics Projects for Young Scientists.* New York: Franklin Watts, 1991.

Stwertka, Albert. *Superconductors: The Irresistible Future.* Venture Books. New York: Franklin Watts, 1991.

MAGAZINES

Popular Mechanics
Box 7170
Red Oak, IA 51591

Popular Science
Box 5100
Harlan, IA 51563

Scientific American
415 Madison Avenue
New York, NY 10017

INDEX